Quick & Easy
Simple Delicious Food Processor and Blender Recipes

Acknowledgments

I believe that I am the most fortunate person I know. I have the career of my dreams, working with and for the nicest people I have ever met. Doing these books is a dream come true for me and I would like to thank everyone who helped along the way.

First and foremost, my family. I have been blessed with a devoted husband Martin, incredible daughter Nevar, loving stepson Gerry and precious grandchildren, Brennan and Patrick who give me so much joy. I have the best mom in the world Yvette, my Dad Reggie, who always gives me terrific recipe ideas and my sister Gail who helps getting me organized, which is quite a task.

Next, I need to thank you Wolfgang. You are the real deal. A finer person or chef, in my opinion there will never be. I adore working with you and learning from you. Your have an unsurpassed work ethic as well as passion for excellence and teaching. These past 10 years have been a glorious dream. Thanks for all you have made possible in my life.

My deepest thanks to Jonathan Schwartz who has developed these books and worked so hard to make them of incredible quality as well as very affordable. Thank you to Syd Silverman who continues to be the best boss that anyone could ask for. Thank you to Mike Sanseverino for manufacturing these brilliant electric products for me and the world. They make us all better cooks.

Thank you so much to all of our WP customers. I appreciate all your support, emails and suggestions. God Bless you all.

Daniel Koren, my genius who lays out these books and edits so patiently with me.
Chris Davis, my brilliant photographer and his assistant Erica Taylor. Thank you Trace Ferguson for your creative art direction. A special thank you to my daughter Nevar. You worked so hard on this project with me, designing shots, picking recipes, food styling and organizing. This was my favorite book to do because of you. You are the best daughter and you are so talented. Thank you to Nevar's wonderful assistant Michael Alberts, my best friend Lori Bain, Ann Marie Shuta who gave me the Gluten-Free Pizza recipe and Doris Boerst who gave me the German Cole Slaw recipe.

Today the food processor is almost as common in the kitchen as a toaster oven. My food processor is perfect for shredding, slicing and mixing ingredients. It is the perfect tool for making salsa, pesto, salad dressings, grinding meats and even making pizza dough. Shredding cheese or making whipped cream, the food processor makes preparation so much faster and better.

Debra Murray has been my assistant at the Home Shopping Network for over ten years and I know her passion for cooking using quality appliances to make anyone a better cook. Debra knows how to use the food processor to its maximum ability. Her passion for cooking and experimental nature created this amazing collection of recipes. I have urged her to share them with as many people as possible with this book.

An extremely talented cook, Debra shares my WELL (Wolfgang's Eat, Love, Live!™) philosophy of good cooking and warm hospitality. I believe everyone should use the freshest, all-natural ingredients, locally grown, organic when possible and raised using sustainable humane methods. I learned long ago, beside my mother and grandmother, one should always put lots of love into cooking. Debra does just that, which is evident in this book.

Table Of Contents

Getting Started

Page 9

Soups & Salads

Page 48

Crusts, Pizzas & Doughs

Meats

Drinks & Shakes

Desserts

Food Processor & Blender Tips

My food processor has made me a better cook. I has helped me make food from scratch, which is healthier for my friends and family. It is also much less expensive than buying prepared sauces or foods which are filled with additives and preservatives.

Chopping, slicing, dicing, kneading, pureeing, my food processor is always ready to take on any task. From Mousses to ice cream to grinding my own meats, the food processor is one of the most versatile appliances. I hope these tips will help you make the most out of your food processor and blender.

Different Food Processor Models

Over the years, Wolfgang Puck has sold various food processor models. Every model is a bit different so use this book as a guideline rather than exact directions. All of the food processor recipes will work without adjustments in a 7, 11 or 12 cup food processor. If you have purchased a 4 cup food processor or have the chopper bowl for the immersion blender, the ingredients of each recipe need to be reduced by half.

Blender

The blender recipes work for all blender models. Remember to keep your hand on the lid when using the blender.

Immersion Blender

You can use an immersion blender with many of the recipes. When using the immersion blender, place the ingredients into a deep bowl, carafe or pot depending on the recipe and blend in that particular container. Remember to reduce the ingredients in each recipe by half.

Blades

Use extreme caution when handling or cleaning any of the blades as they are extremely sharp. Never place blades in a sink full of water or on the top shelf of the dishwasher. Should you have difficulty removing the metal S blade, simply turn the bowl upside down and lightly tap it on the counter to loosen the blade without having to touch it.

Preparation

I recommend to gather all the ingredients before preparing a particular recipe. When using a food processor, things happen fast and it will make your cooking much easier having all the ingredients ready and within reach.

Consistency

Many recipes such as salsas or soups can be processed to a desired consistency. For best results, use the pulse button until you achieve your desired consistency.

Chopping

Always cut the food into even pieces before chopping. For instance, an onion should be cut into four equal pieces. Doing so will allow for the onion to get evenly chopped.

Slicing

To achieve even slicing, fill the feed tube with as much food as possible. For instance, instead of pushing two long carrots through the feed tube, I cut them into 4 pieces so that the feed tube is full. You will have perfect slices this way.

Avoid Excessive Pressure

Do not exert pressure on whatever you are slicing or shredding. Simply hold the pusher on the food in the feed tube and push lightly. Excessive pressure will not increase the speed of preparation and only bend your blade.

Breads and Doughs

When making bread or pizza dough, only get a portion of the water to lukewarm temperature (110 degrees) just enough to dissolve the yeast. The remaining water should be ice cold water. When forming a dough ball in the in food processor, the dough gets hot. If it gets too hot, you will not get a rise. Stay with the machine while processing, don't let the processing time exceed two minutes.

Atmosphere & Altitude

If you find that a dough ball does not form properly or that ice cream does not purée properly, your location may have a lot to do with it. Always measure exactly but keep a small amount of extra water when making bread or pasta dough and extra cream when making ice cream.

Emulsion

When making an emulsion, always let the ingredients process well before slowly adding the oil through the feed tube.

Cheesecake

When making cheesecake, always stop the processing and scrape the bowl several times to ensure that all ingredients are evenly combined. Remember to let the blades come to a complete stop before opening the lid.

Ice Cream and Sorbet

When making ice cream or sorbet, always add the liquid through the feed tube. Do not add it with the frozen fruit as it may cause the food to freeze to the blade.

Meat

When grinding meat, always season the meat before grinding.

Soup

Let the soup cool before adding it to the food processor or blender. Don't fill your food processor or blender past the halfway mark and process in batches to achieve even consistency.

Smoothies and Frozen Drinks

For smoothies and frozen drinks, add the liquid and soft ingredients to the blender first then add the frozen fruit or ice.

Getting Started

Crunchy Ranch Chips

Ingredients:

4 Yukon gold potatoes, washed

4 cups peanut oil

1 envelope (1 ounce) ranch dip seasoning

Sea salt

1. Fill a large bowl with water.
2. Set the slicing disk to the thinnest setting and fit it into the food processor.
3. Secure lid.
4. With the food processor running, push potatoes through the feed tube.
5. Transfer potato slices to the water bowl.
6. Preheat oil in a stockpot over medium heat.
7. Using a thermometer, measure the oil temperature until it reaches 350 degrees.
8. Remove 12 potato slices from the water and pat them dry using paper towels.
9. Carefully place potato slices into the oil using a skimmer or slotted spoon.
10. Fry for 2 minutes or until desired color; move chips frequently while frying.
11. Remove chips from oil and drain them on paper towels.
12. Lightly sprinkle ranch dip seasoning and a touch of salt over the chips.
13. Repeat with remaining potato slices; make sure oil reaches 350 degrees before adding another batch of potatoes.
14. Serve.

Dry Beef Cheese Ball

Ingredients:

1 package (8 ounces) cream cheese

1 envelope (1 ounce) ranch dip seasoning

1 package (3 ounces) dried beef, divided

1 package (8 ounces) sharp cheddar cheese

1. Fit food processor with the metal S blade.
2. Place the cream cheese, ranch seasoning and half of the beef into the food processor.
3. With the metal S blade still in place, add the shredding disk (large hole side up) to the food processor; secure lid.
4. With the food processor running, push the cheese through the feed tube.
5. Continue to process for 1 minute.
6. Chop the remaining beef with a knife to make small squares.
7. Place beef squares onto a piece of plastic wrap.
8. Shape cheese mixture into a ball and place it in the center of the plastic wrap.
9. Roll ball over the beef pieces until it is covered with beef pieces.
10. Wrap and chill for 2 hours before serving.

Deb's Tip:

The dried beef can be found in the cold cut section of your grocery store. You can also try deli ham instead of dried beef.

Herb Cheese Ball

Ingredients:

1 package (8 ounces) cream cheese

2 ounces feta cheese

2 ounces bleu cheese

1 teaspoon sea salt

½ teaspoon garlic salt

1 teaspoon freshly ground pepper

10 basil leaves

½ teaspoon rosemary

1 tablespoon green onions, chopped

1. Fit food processor with the metal S blade.
2. Place all ingredients into the food processor; secure lid and process for 30 seconds.
3. Scrape the sides using a rubber spatula, secure lid and pulse 3 times.
4. Transfer the mixture onto the center of a piece of plastic wrap.
5. Wrap the mixture in the plastic wrap and form it into a ball.
6. Refrigerate for 2 hours before serving.

Deb's Tip:
Roll cheese ball in toasted walnuts then serve it with apple slices, pear slices as well as crackers.

Cheese Ball with Pecans

Ingredients:

1 package (8 ounces) extra sharp cheddar cheese

1 package (8 ounces) cream cheese

1 shallot, peeled

1 red bell pepper, seeds removed

1 teaspoon lemon juice

1 teaspoon Louisiana hot sauce

1 cup pecan pieces

1. Fit food processor with the shredding disk (large hole side up) and secure lid.
2. With the food processor running, push cheddar cheese through the feed tube.
3. Replace the shredding disk with the metal S blade.
4. Add cream cheese, shallot and bell pepper to the food processor; secure lid.
5. Process until smooth.
6. Add lemon juice and hot sauce to the food processor.
7. Secure lid and pulse to incorporate.
8. Form the cheese mixture into a ball.
9. Spread pecans on a sheet of plastic wrap.
10. Roll ball over the pecans until it is covered with pecans.
11. Wrap ball in plastic wrap until ready to serve.

Deviled Eggs

Ingredients:

12 hard boiled eggs, peeled and halved

¼ cup mayonnaise

2 ounces cream cheese

4 tablespoons unsalted butter, at room temperature

½ teaspoon salt

½ teaspoon freshly ground pepper

½ teaspoon red pepper sauce

¼ teaspoon dry mustard

1. Fit food processor with the metal S blade.
2. Remove yolks from the eggs and set aside egg whites.
3. In the food processor, combine egg yolks and remaining ingredients, except egg whites; secure lid and purée until smooth.
4. Transfer mixture to a pastry bag and refrigerate for 2 hours.
5. Cut off the tip of the pastry bag and fill each egg white half with the mixture.
6. Serve immediately.

Deb's Tip:
Garnish with olive slices, jumbo lump crab meat or caviar.

Ceviche

Ingredients:

1 cup fresh lime juice, divided

1 teaspoon salt

1 pound fresh sea scallops, sliced thin horizontally

2 garlic cloves

1 small onion

1 Serrano chile pepper, seeds and membrane removed

¼ cup fresh cilantro leaves

1. In a bowl, combine ½ cup of lime juice and salt.
2. Place scallops into the bowl and let marinate overnight.
3. Drain the scallops.
4. Toss scallops in remaining lime juice; set aside.
5. Fit the food processor with the metal S blade.
6. Place remaining ingredients into the food processor and secure lid.
7. Pulse 6 times to chop evenly.
8. Transfer mixture to the bowl with the scallops and chill for 1 hour before serving.

Deb's Tip:
Serve in a glass over fresh lettuce leaves.

Salsa Shrimp Dip

Ingredients:

1 pint grape tomatoes

2 green onions (white part only)

1 garlic clove

1 Serrano Chile, seeds and membrane removed

Juice and zest from 1 lime

2 tablespoons cilantro leaves

½ teaspoon kosher salt

1 teaspoon extra-virgin olive oil

1 pound cooked medium shrimp, shells removed

1 small avocado, diced small

1. Fit the food processor with the metal S blade.
2. Place all ingredients, except shrimp and avocado, into the food processor.
3. Secure lid and pulse 5 times to chop; do not purée.
4. Transfer mixture to a bowl.
5. Chop the shrimp into ½-inch pieces and add them to the bowl; mix well.
6. Chill for 1 hour.
7. Top with avocado and serve with tortilla chips for dipping.

Artichoke Dip

Ingredients:

1 piece (3 ounces) Parmesan cheese

1 can (14 ounces) quartered artichokes, drained

1 package (8 ounces) cream cheese

½ cup mayonnaise

1 teaspoon lemon juice

1 teaspoon hot pepper sauce

1 teaspoon garlic salt

1. Preheat broiler.
2. Fit food processor with the shredding disk (small hole side up); secure lid.
3. With the food processor running, push cheese through the feed tube.
4. Replace the shredding disk with the metal S blade.
5. Add remaining ingredients to the food processor; secure lid.
6. Pulse 5 times to incorporate.
7. Transfer mixture to an oven-safe casserole.
8. Place casserole in the oven, 4 inches below the broiler.
9. Broil for 5 minutes or until golden brown.
10. Serve immediately.

Deb's Tip:
Serve with a combination of pita and tortilla chips.

Tzatziki Dip

Ingredients:

1 English cucumber, peeled and sliced lengthwise

5 garlic cloves

4 ounces cream cheese

2 ounces goat cheese

2 cups Greek yogurt

1 teaspoon onion salt

1 teaspoon garlic powder

1 teaspoon black pepper

1 teaspoon fresh dill, chopped

6 fresh mint leaves

1. Using a small spoon, remove the seeds from both sides of the cucumber.
2. Set the slicing disk to 1mm and fit it in the food processor; secure lid.
3. With the food processor running, push the cucumber through the feed tube.
4. Transfer cucumber slices to a strainer to drain excess liquid.
5. Replace the slicing disk with the metal S blade.
6. Place the cucumber slices and garlic into the food processor.
7. Secure lid and pulse 5 times.
8. Add remaining ingredients to the food processor and secure lid.
9. Pulse 6 times to incorporate.
10. Chill until ready to serve.

Hummus

Ingredients:

1 can (16 ounces) chickpeas, drained, liquid reserved

3 garlic cloves

1 teaspoon cumin

1 tablespoon fresh lemon juice

1 teaspoon salt

½ teaspoon cayenne pepper

1. Fit food processor with the metal S blade.
2. Place all ingredients, except chickpea liquid, into the food processor.
3. Secure lid and purée for 1 minute, then slowly drizzle the liquid through the feed tube until well incorporated.

White Bean Cilantro Hummus

Ingredients:

1 can (15 ounces) northern white beans, drained

1 tablespoon Tahini paste

1 tablespoon fresh lemon juice

2 garlic cloves

1 teaspoon cumin

½ teaspoon cayenne pepper

2 tablespoons safflower oil

1 tablespoon cilantro leaves

1. Fit food processor with the metal S blade.
2. Add all ingredients, except oil and cilantro, to the food processor.
3. Secure lid and process until smooth.
4. With the food processor running, drizzle oil through the feed tube.
5. Add cilantro to the food processor; secure lid and pulse to incorporate.
6. Serve with pita chips.

Fresh Salsa

Ingredients:

1 pint grape tomatoes

1 mild chile pepper, seeds removed

1 small sweet onion

2 whole garlic cloves

1 tomatillo, husk removed

1 bundle cilantro, stems removed

2 tablespoons fresh lime juice

1½ teaspoons kosher salt

1 can (10¾ ounces) Mexican tomatoes with lime and cilantro

1. Fit food processor with the metal S blade.
2. Place all ingredients into the food processor; secure lid and pulse until desired consistency.
3. Taste for seasoning and serve with your favorite chips.

Guacamole

Ingredients:

3 garlic cloves

3 green onions

½ cup fresh cilantro leaves, chopped

2 large avocados, pitted

1 Poblano chile, seeds and membrane removed

1 teaspoon salt

½ teaspoon freshly ground pepper

Juice from 1 large lime

1. Fit food processor with the metal S blade.
2. Place all ingredients into the food processor; secure lid and pulse until desired consistency.
3. Serve chilled with my fresh salsa and your favorite chips.

Tapenade

Ingredients:

½ cup oil-brined olives, pitted

½ cup stuffed green olives

3 garlic cloves

2 anchovies

1 roasted red pepper

1 tablespoon capers

1 teaspoon extra-virgin olive oil

1. Fit food processor with the metal S blade.
2. Place all ingredients into the food processor and secure lid.
3. Pulse until desired consistency.

Sundried Tomato Dip

Ingredients:

4 ounces cream cheese

1 container (6.5 ounces) garlic & herb spread

½ cup mayonnaise

8 ounces sundried tomatoes, drained and chopped

5 artichoke hearts, chopped

6 basil leaves

½ teaspoon salt

½ teaspoon pepper

1. Fit food processor with the metal S blade.
2. Place cream cheese, herb spread and mayonnaise into the food processor; secure lid.
3. Process for 1 minute or until smooth.
4. Add remaining ingredients to the food processor; secure lid.
5. Pulse to combine and serve.

Nectarine Salsa

Ingredients:

3 nectarines, pits removed with skins on

1 small red bell pepper

2 green onions

1 Serrano chile pepper, seeds and membrane removed

1 tablespoon fresh cilantro

1 teaspoon honey

Juice and zest from 1 lime

1. Fit food processor with the metal S blade.
2. Place all ingredients into the food processor and secure lid.
3. Pulse 6 times or until all ingredients are evenly chopped.
4. Chill until ready to serve.

Salsa Verde

Ingredients:

2 Poblano chile peppers, diced

8 tomatillos, peeled and quartered

1 garlic clove

1 small onion, quartered

2 cups chicken stock

1 teaspoon cumin seeds

1 teaspoon salt

¼ cup fresh cilantro

1 tablespoon fresh lime juice

1. In a saucepan over medium heat, combine all ingredients, except cilantro and lime juice; cook for 20 minutes or until tender and let cool.
2. Fit food processor with the metal S blade.
3. Place mixture and remaining ingredients into food processor; secure lid.
4. Purée until smooth.

Potato Pancakes

Makes 1 serving

Ingredients:

1 large Russet potato, washed and peeled

2 tablespoons extra-virgin olive oil

½ teaspoon salt

1. Cut potato into pieces and soak it in a bowl of water.
2. Fit food processor with the shredding disk (large hole side up); secure lid.
3. With the food processor running, push potatoes through the feed tube.
4. Transfer potatoes to paper towels and pat them dry.
5. Preheat oil in a sauté pan over medium heat.
6. Add potatoes to the pan and cook for 4 minutes.
7. Using a rubber spatula, lift the corner to make sure the bottom is evenly browned.
8. Flip pancake using the spatula and cook for an additional 4 minutes.
9. Season pancakes with salt and serve.

Deb's Tip:
This is amazing topped with sour cream and smoked salmon.

Smoked Salmon Stuffed Tomatoes

Ingredients:

1 shallot, peeled
6 ounces smoked salmon, thinly sliced
4 ounces cream cheese
2 tablespoons unsalted butter
4 fresh dill sprigs
20 cherry tomatoes

1. Set the slicing disk to its thinnest setting and fit it in the food processor.
2. Secure lid.
3. With the food processor running, push shallot through the feed tube.
4. Remove shallots and set aside.
5. Replace the slicing disk with the metal S blade.
6. Add salmon, cream cheese and butter to the food processor.
7. Secure lid and process until smooth.
8. Add dill sprigs to the food processor and secure lid; pulse to incorporate.
9. Transfer mixture to a pastry bag.
10. Using a paring knife, slice the bottom of each tomato so the tomatoes sit flat.
11. Cut a hole in the top of each tomato and scoop out the seeds.
12. Using the pastry bag, fill each tomato with the smoked salmon filling.
13. Top each tomato with a shallot slice and serve.

Buffalo Chicken Lettuce Wraps

Ingredients:

1 carrot, peeled

2 green onions

1 celery stalk

3 boneless, skinless chicken breasts

1 tablespoon extra-virgin olive oil

1 tablespoon salted butter

2 tablespoons Louisiana hot sauce

1 teaspoon soy sauce

1 teaspoon cider vinegar

½ tablespoon ketchup

½ cup bleu cheese, crumbled

1 head bibb lettuce

1. Fit food processor with the shredding disk (large hole side up) and secure lid.
2. With the food processor running, push carrot through the feed tube.
3. Transfer carrots to a bowl.
4. Replace shredding disk with the metal S blade.
5. Add green onions and celery to the food processor; secure lid and pulse to chop.
6. Transfer green onions and celery to the bowl with the carrots.
7. Place chicken into the food processor.
8. Secure lid and process for 30 seconds.
9. Heat oil in a sauté pan over medium heat.
10. Add chicken to the pan and brown; break up the chicken using a spatula.
11. Add butter, hot sauce and soy sauce to the pan; let simmer for 5 minutes.
12. Add vinegar and ketchup to the pan; mix well.
13. Remove pan from heat.
14. Transfer pan contents to a serving bowl; add carrot mixture and top with cheese.
15. Place lettuce leaves around the bowl.
16. Place 1 tablespoon of chicken mixture in the center of each leaf, roll up and eat it like a taco.

Tomato Tart

Crust:

¾ cup all purpose flour

¾ cup cornmeal

¼ cup Parmesan cheese, grated

1 large egg

½ cup salted butter, cut into pieces

Filling:

½ cup Swiss cheese, shredded

3 large eggs

1 cup heavy cream

1 teaspoon salt

1 teaspoon freshly ground pepper

1 large tomato, sliced

4 basil leaves, chopped

1. Preheat oven to 350 degrees.
2. Fit food processor with the metal S blade.
3. Place flour, cornmeal and Parmesan cheese into the food processor; secure lid.
4. Pulse to combine.
5. Drop the egg and butter through the feed tube and pulse to combine then process for 30 seconds until crumbly.
6. Press mixture into a 9-inch fluted tart pan.
7. Cover the pan with parchment paper and place pie weights on top of the paper.
8. Bake in the oven for 14 minutes.
9. Remove pie weights and parchment paper.
10. Top the crust with Swiss cheese.
11. Place remaining ingredients, except tomato and basil, into the food processor.
12. Secure lid and process.
13. Pour mixture into the crust and top with tomato slices.
14. Bake in the oven for 35 minutes then let cool for 10 minutes.
15. Remove tart from the pan, top with basil and serve.

Gazpacho

Ingredients:

5 ripe Roma tomatoes

1 medium yellow bell pepper, seeded

1 medium sweet onion, quartered

1 English cucumber

¼ cup flat leaf parsley

2 tablespoons balsamic vinegar

1 teaspoon salt

½ teaspoon pepper

¼ cup tomato juice

¼ cup extra-virgin olive oil

1. Fit food processor with the metal S blade.
2. Place all ingredients, except oil, into the food processor; secure lid.
3. With the food processor running, drizzle oil through the feed tube.
4. Chill until ready to serve.

Peanut Butter

Ingredients:

2 cups roasted peanuts

2 tablespoons brown sugar

¼ teaspoon salt

2 tablespoons peanut oil

1. Fit food processor with the metal S blade.
2. Place all ingredients, except oil, into the food processor; secure lid.
3. With the food processor running, drizzle oil through the feed tube.
4. Total processing time is 2 minutes.

Basil Pesto

Ingredients:

1 piece (1 ounce) Parmesan Cheese

3 garlic cloves, preferably roasted

½ teaspoon freshly ground pepper

3 tablespoons unsalted butter

2 cups fresh basil leaves

½ cup spinach leaves

¼ cup pine nuts

¼ cup extra-virgin olive oil

1. Fit food processor with the grating disk; secure lid.
2. With the food processor running, push cheese through the feed tube.
3. Replace grating disk with the metal S blade.
4. Add remaining ingredients, except oil, to the food processor; secure lid.
5. With the food processor running, slowly drizzle the oil through the feed tube.
6. Serve.

Mayonnaise

Ingredients:

2 large egg yolks

1 teaspoon mustard

2 teaspoons white vinegar

½ teaspoon salt

1 cup safflower oil

1. Fit food processor with the metal S blade.
2. Place all ingredients, except oil, into the food processor; secure lid.
3. With the food processor running, drizzle oil through the feed tube; process until well incorporated.

Thousand Island Dressing

Ingredients:

1 cup mayonnaise

2 teaspoons tomato paste

1 hard cooked egg

6 stuffed olives

2 small pickles

1 teaspoon lemon juice

1 shallot, peeled

1 teaspoon paprika

1 teaspoon sugar

1. Fit food processor with the metal S blade.
2. Place all ingredients into the food processor and secure lid.
3. Pulse until evenly combined.

Orange Poppy Seed Dressing

Ingredients:

1 navel orange, quartered
1 tablespoon honey
2 tablespoons rice wine vinegar
2 teaspoons poppy seeds

½ teaspoon salt
2 green onions
½ cup safflower oil

1. Fit food processor with the metal S blade.
2. Place all ingredients, except oil, into the food processor; secure lid.
3. With the food processor running, drizzle oil through the feed tube; process until well incorporated.

French Dressing

Ingredients:

⅓ cup red wine vinegar
2 garlic cloves
1 shallot, peeled
1 teaspoon salt
1 teaspoon paprika

1 tablespoon yellow mustard
2 tablespoons ketchup
1 large egg
⅔ cup safflower oil

1. Fit food processor with the metal S blade.
2. Place all ingredients, except oil, into the food processor; secure lid.
3. With the food processor running, drizzle oil through the feed tube; process until well incorporated.

Bleu Cheese Dressing

Ingredients:

8 ounces bleu cheese, divided

1 teaspoon red wine vinegar

1 teaspoon lemon juice

½ cup mayonnaise

½ teaspoon freshly ground pepper

½ teaspoon fresh parsley, chopped

1. Place 4 ounces bleu cheese and vinegar into a microwave-safe bowl.
2. Microwave for 30 seconds or until cheese is melted.
3. Fit food processor with the metal S blade.
4. Place bleu cheese and remaining ingredients into the food processor.
5. Secure lid and pulse until combined.

Caesar Dressing

Ingredients:

2 garlic cloves

¼ cup Parmesan cheese, grated

1 tablespoon fresh lemon juice

1 large egg

1 teaspoon Worcestershire sauce

½ teaspoon Dijon mustard

½ teaspoon freshly ground pepper

3 whole anchovy filets

⅔ cup extra-virgin olive oil

1. Fit food processor with the metal S blade.
2. Place all ingredients, except oil, into the food processor.
3. Secure lid and process for 1 minute.
4. With the food processor running, drizzle oil through the feed tube; process until well incorporated.

41

Homemade Butter

Makes ½ pound

Ingredients:

1 pint heavy cream
3 ice cubes

1. Fit food processor with the metal S blade.
2. Pour cream into the food processor and secure lid.
3. Process for 4 minutes or until cream turns to curds.
4. Place a fine mesh strainer over a bowl.
5. Scrape food processor contents into the strainer, including the liquid.
6. Using a rubber spatula, press butter to extract all the liquid.
7. Place butter back into the food processor and add the ice cubes.
8. Secure lid and process for 1 minute.
9. Place the strainer over another bowl and strain all the liquid.
10. Place butter into an airtight container and refrigerate.

Deb's Tip:
Save the liquid extracted in step six, it is a wonderful buttermilk.

Steak Butter

Ingredients:

2 tablespoons dry white wine

1 shallot, peeled minced

1 garlic clove, minced

1 teaspoon kosher salt

1 teaspoon freshly cracked pepper

1 tablespoon parsley leaves

½ cup butter, at room temperature

1. In a saucepan over medium heat, combine wine, shallot, garlic, salt and pepper.
2. Simmer for 3 minutes or until the garlic and shallot are cooked through and most of the wine has evaporated; remove from heat and let cool.
3. Fit food processor with the metal S blade.
4. Add saucepan mixture, parsley and butter to the food processor; secure lid.
5. Pulse to incorporate.
6. Scrape mixture onto a piece of plastic wrap.
7. Shape butter into a log and cover it with plastic wrap.
8. Refrigerate until ready to use.

Deb's Tip:
Right after taking your steak off the grill, spread this butter on both sides of your steak.

Cilantro Lime Butter

Makes ½ cup

Ingredients:

1 large lime, juice and zest

2 garlic cloves, minced

1 teaspoon salt

½ teaspoon red pepper flakes

½ cup salted butter

1 tablespoon green onions

2 tablespoons fresh cilantro leaves

1. In a saucepan over medium heat, combine lime juice and garlic.
2. Let simmer for 1 minute or until garlic is tender.
3. Add salt and pepper flakes to the pan and let cool.
4. Fit food processor with the metal S blade.
5. Add garlic mixture, zest and butter to the food processor; secure lid.
6. Process until smooth.
7. Add remaining ingredients to food processor; secure lid and pulse to incorporate.
8. Transfer butter onto a piece of plastic wrap.
9. Shape butter into a log and cover it with plastic wrap.
10. Refrigerate until ready to use.

Deb's Tip:
I love to grill swordfish or salmon in my panini maker and top it with this butter after removing it from the heat.

Strawberry Butter

Ingredients:

2 cups heavy cream

4 ice cubes

3 tablespoons powdered sugar

6 ripe strawberries

1 teaspoon strawberry extract (optional)

1. Fit food processor with the metal S blade.
2. Pour cream into the food processor and secure lid.
3. Process for 4 minutes or until cream turns to curds.
4. Place a fine mesh strainer over a bowl.
5. Scrape food processor contents into the strainer, including the liquid.
6. Using a rubber spatula, press butter to extract all the liquid.
7. Place the butter back into the food processor and add the ice cubes.
8. Secure lid and process for 2 minutes or until butter becomes solid.
9. Drain the liquid and place the butter back into the food processor.
10. Add remaining ingredients to the food processor and secure lid.
11. Process for 1 minute.
12. Drain the liquid and store the butter in an airtight container in the refrigerator.

Deb's Tip:
Top a homemade scone or Belgian waffle with this butter. Delicious!

Honey Almond Butter

Ingredients:

2 cups blanched almonds

3 tablespoons honey

3 tablespoons safflower oil

1. Fit food processor with the metal S blade.
2. Place almonds and honey into the food processor; secure lid.
3. With the food processor running, drizzle oil through the feed tube.
4. Process for 3 minutes.

Balsamic Fig Butter

Ingredients:

3 tablespoons balsamic vinegar

4 dried figs

1 teaspoon kosher salt

½ teaspoon fennel seeds

½ cup unsalted butter

1. In a saucepan, combine vinegar and figs; bring to a simmer.
2. Add salt and fennel to the saucepan; remove from heat and let cool.
3. Fit food processor with the metal S blade.
4. Add fig mixture and butter to the food processor; secure lid.
5. Pulse 6 times to incorporate.
6. Transfer butter onto a piece of plastic wrap and roll it into a log.
7. Cover with plastic wrap and refrigerate until ready to use.

Soups & Salads

Broccoli Cheddar Soup

Ingredients:

1 medium onion, peeled and quartered

2 tablespoons extra-virgin olive oil

1 head of broccoli

1½ cups chicken stock

½ teaspoon salt

½ teaspoon freshly ground pepper

1 teaspoon lemon juice

1 teaspoon hot pepper sauce

1 piece (4 ounces) cheddar cheese

1. Fit food processor with the metal S blade.
2. Place onions into the food processor and secure lid; pulse to chop.
3. Heat oil in a stockpot over medium heat.
4. Add onions to the stockpot and cook until tender.
5. Place broccoli into the food processor and secure lid; pulse to chop.
6. Transfer broccoli to the stockpot.
7. Add stock, salt and pepper to the stockpot; bring to a boil and cook for 5 minutes.
8. Reduce the heat.
9. Add lemon juice and hot sauce to the stockpot; let cook for 10 minutes.
10. Replace metal S blade with the shredding disk (large hole side up); secure lid.
11. With the food processor running, push cheese through the feed tube.
12. Add the cheese to the soup.
13. Replace shredding disk with the metal S blade.
14. Divide soup and pour it into the food processor; secure lid.
15. Purée soup until desired consistency.
16. Repeat with remaining soup and serve.

Carrot Coriander Soup

Ingredients:

1 medium onion, quartered

1 piece (½ inch) fresh ginger, peeled

2 tablespoons unsalted butter

2 pounds carrots, peeled

4 cups chicken stock

1 cup water

1 teaspoon coriander seeds

½ teaspoon salt

½ teaspoon ground white pepper

½ cup heavy cream

1 tablespoon cilantro leaves

1. Fit food processor with the metal S blade.
2. Add onions and ginger to the food processor; secure lid and pulse to chop.
3. Melt butter in a stockpot over medium heat.
4. Add onion mixture to stockpot and cook for 2 minutes or until tender; do not brown.
5. Replace the metal S blade with the slicing disk set to 3mm; secure lid.
6. With the food processor running, push carrots through the feed tube.
7. Add carrots, stock, water, coriander, salt and pepper to the stockpot.
8. Let simmer for 20 minutes.
9. Add heavy cream to the stockpot.
10. Remove from heat and let cool for 10 minutes.
11. Replace the slicing disk with the metal S blade.
12. Divide the soup and pour it into the food processor; secure lid.
13. Purée soup until desired consistency.
14. Repeat with remaining soup.
15. Serve hot or cold topped with cilantro leaves.

Cream of Spinach Soup

Ingredients:

2 tablespoons unsalted butter

1 medium onion, chopped

3 tablespoons all purpose flour

2 cups chicken stock

1 bag (10 ounces) baby spinach leaves

¼ teaspoon salt

½ teaspoon ground white pepper

¼ teaspoon nutmeg

1 package (8 ounces) cream cheese

8 fresh basil leaves

1. Melt butter in a stockpot over medium heat.
2. Add onions to the stockpot and cook until tender; do not brown.
3. Stir in the flour and mix until smooth.
4. Whisk the stock into the flour mixture; stir until smooth.
5. Add spinach, salt, pepper and nutmeg to the stockpot; cook for 10 minutes.
6. Remove from heat and let cool.
7. Pour soup into the food processor.
8. Add remaining ingredients to the food processor and secure lid.
9. Purée until desired consistency and serve.

Tomato Soup

Ingredients:

1 small onion, peeled

1 carrot, peeled

2 celery stalks

2 garlic cloves

2 tablespoons unsalted butter

1 can (28 ounces) tomatoes in juice

2 sprigs thyme

1 teaspoon salt

½ teaspoon freshly ground pepper

2 cups chicken stock

1. Fit the food processor with the metal S blade.
2. Place the onion, carrot, celery and garlic into the food processor; pulse to chop.
3. Melt the butter in a stockpot over medium heat.
4. Add the onion mixture to the stockpot.
5. Divide the tomatoes.
6. Place tomatoes into the food processor and secure lid; pulse to chop.
7. Repeat with remaining tomatoes.
8. Stir chopped tomatoes into the stockpot with the onion mixture.
9. Add thyme, salt and pepper to the stockpot; stir and cook for 15 minutes.
10. Add chicken stock to the stockpot; stir and let simmer for 20 additional minutes.
11. Pour soup into the food processor; secure lid and purée until desired consistency.
12. Serve immediately.

Italian Wedding Soup

Meatball Ingredients:

½ cup heavy cream

1 piece (6 inches) crusty French bread

1 small onion

1 large egg

2 garlic cloves

8 ounces lean beef chunks

8 ounces lean pork chunks

1 piece (3 ounces) Parmesan cheese

2 tablespoons flat leaf parsley

1 tablespoon salt

½ tablespoon freshly ground pepper

Soup Ingredients:

12 cups chicken stock

1 pound spinach leaves, chopped

2 large eggs

Salt and pepper to taste

1. In a large stockpot, bring chicken stock to a boil.
2. Fit food processor with the metal S blade.
3. Add heavy cream and bread to the food processor; secure lid.
4. Pulse 3 times to combine.
5. Add onion, egg, garlic, beef and pork to the food processor; secure lid.
6. Pulse 3 times to combine.
7. With the metal S blade still in place, add the grating disk to the food processor and secure lid.
8. With the food processor running, push the cheese through the feed tube.
9. Remove the grating disk and add the parsley, salt and pepper; secure lid.
10. Pulse 3 times to combine.
11. Form mixture into 1-inch meatballs.
12. Add meatballs and spinach to the boiling chicken stock; cook for 9 minutes.
13. In a bowl, whisk the eggs.
14. While stirring the soup in a circular motion using a fork, drizzle eggs into the moving stock until thin egg strands form.
15. Taste for seasoning and serve with additional grated cheese.

Potato Leek Soup

Makes 4 to 6 servings

Ingredients:

3 medium leeks (white part only), rinsed and split lengthwise

1 pound Yukon gold potatoes, washed

2 tablespoons unsalted butter

4 cups chicken stock

1 teaspoon kosher salt

1 teaspoon freshly ground pepper

1 package (8 ounces) cream cheese

½ cup milk

1 teaspoon fresh chives, chopped

1. Set the slicing disk to 3mm and fit it into the food processor; secure lid.
2. With the food processor running, push leeks through the feed tube.
3. Remove leeks and set aside; secure lid.
4. With the food processor running, push potatoes through the feed tube.
5. Melt butter in a stockpot over medium heat.
6. Add leeks and potatoes to the stockpot.
7. Add stock, salt and pepper to the stockpot and cook for 30 minutes.
8. Add remaining ingredients, except chives, to the stockpot.
9. Replace the slicing disk with the metal S blade.
10. Divide soup and pour it into food processor; secure lid.
11. Purée soup until desired consistency.
12. Repeat with remaining soup.
13. Garnish with chives and serve hot or cold.

Santa Fe Salad with Chicken

Makes 2 servings

Chicken:

2 boneless, skinless chicken breasts

1 tablespoon extra-virgin olive oil

1 teaspoon salt

½ teaspoon freshly ground pepper

½ teaspoon paprika

Cilantro Lime Dressing:

3 limes, juice and zest

2 garlic cloves, peeled

2 teaspoons grown cumin

2 teaspoons grown coriander

2 tablespoons cilantro leaves

½ teaspoon salt

¼ teaspoon freshly ground pepper

½ cup extra-virgin olive oil

Salad:

3 green onions (white part only)

1 red bell pepper, seeded

8 grape tomatoes

¼ cup cilantro

½ cup black beans, cooked

½ cup corn kernels

2 cups lettuce, shredded

¼ cup pepper jack cheese, shredded

1. Preheat grill.
2. Wash and pat dry the chicken.
3. Rub chicken with oil.
4. Season chicken with salt, pepper and paprika.
5. Grill chicken for 10 minutes on each side, cut it into 1-inch cubes and set aside.
6. Fit food processor with the metal S blade.
7. Place green onions, bell pepper, tomatoes and cilantro into the food processor.
8. Secure lid and pulse 4 times.
9. Place mixture into a large bowl.
10. Add beans, corn, lettuce and cheese to the bowl.
11. Place all dressing ingredients, except oil, into the food processor; secure lid.
12. With the food processor running, drizzle oil through the feed tube.
13. Add dressing to the bowl with the salad and toss well.
14. Add chicken to the salad and serve on chilled plates.

Tarragon Turkey Salad

Makes 4 servings

Ingredients:

2 cups cooked turkey, chopped

1 shallot, peeled

2 celery stalks

10 fresh tarragon leaves

⅓ cup mayonnaise

½ teaspoon celery salt

¼ teaspoon freshly ground pepper

4 lettuce leaves, such as radicchio

2 tablespoons pomegranate seeds (optional)

1. Fit food processor with the metal S blade.
2. Place the turkey, shallot, celery and tarragon into the food processor; secure lid.
3. Pulse 3 times.
4. Add mayonnaise, celery salt and pepper to the food processor; secure lid.
5. Pulse 3 times or until uniform chunks are achieved.
6. Scoop mixture into the center of each lettuce leaf.
7. Top with pomegranate seeds and serve.

Ahi Tuna Poke Salad

Makes 4 to 6 servings

Poke Ingredients:

1 pound fresh ahi tuna, cut into ½-inch pieces

½ cup Ponzu (citrus-flavored soy sauce)

1 teaspoon sriracha

2 tablespoons mayonnaise

Salad Ingredients:

1 English cucumber, cut lengthwise

1 teaspoon fresh ginger, minced

1 teaspoon soy sauce

2 teaspoons rice vinegar

½ teaspoon freshly ground pepper

1 tablespoon sesame oil

½ teaspoon black sesame seeds

1. In a bowl, combine all Poke ingredients; toss well and refrigerate.
2. Using a melon baller, scrape and discard the inside of the cucumber slices.
3. Set the slicing disk to 1mm and fit it into the food processor; secure lid.
4. With the food processor running, push cucumber through the feed tube.
5. Transfer cucumbers to paper towels and pat dry.
6. Replace the slicing disk with the metal S blade.
7. Add ginger, soy sauce, rice vinegar and pepper to the food processor; secure lid.
8. With the food processor running, drizzle oil through the feed tube.
9. In a bowl, toss the cucumber with the dressing and sesame seeds; refrigerate.
10. Top cucumber mixture with Poke mixture and serve.

Cucumber Radish Slaw

Ingredients:

1 English cucumber

4 radishes, washed, ends removed

1 small leek, trimmed (white part only)

2 tablespoons cider vinegar

1 tablespoon extra-virgin olive oil

½ teaspoon salt

¼ teaspoon freshly ground pepper

⅛ teaspoon sugar

1. Set the slicing disk to 3mm and fit it into the food processor; secure lid.
2. With the food processor running, push cucumber and radishes through the feed tube.
3. Transfer sliced vegetables to paper towels and pat dry.
4. In a bowl, toss vegetables with remaining ingredients.
5. Serve chilled.

Asian Slaw

Salad Ingredients:

1 head Napa cabbage, sliced

1 red bell pepper, sliced and seeded

1 yellow bell pepper, sliced and seeded

1 small leek, trimmed (white part only)

1 carrot, peeled

1 tablespoon fresh cilantro leaves

1 tablespoon chives, chopped

Dressing Ingredients:

1 piece (¼ inch) ginger, peeled

⅓ cup rice wine vinegar

1 tablespoon soy sauce

½ cup peanut butter

2 tablespoons grape seed oil

2 tablespoons sesame oil

Zest and juice from 1 lime

1 small Serrano pepper, seeds and membranes removed

1. Set the slicing disk to 3mm and fit it into the food processor; secure lid.
2. With the food processor running, push cabbage, bell peppers and leek through the feed tube.
3. Transfer mixture to a large bowl.
4. Replace the slicing disk with the shredding disk (small hole side up); secure lid.
5. With the food processor running, push carrot through the feed tube.
6. Add carrots to the bowl with the cabbage mixture.
7. Replace the slicing disk with the metal S blade.
8. Place all dressing ingredients into the food processor and secure lid; purée.
9. Toss cabbage mixture with the dressing.
10. Top with cilantro and chives.
11. Serve.

Cabbage Slaw with Boiled Dressing

Makes 6 to 8 servings

Ingredients:

1 pound cabbage, cut into pieces

4 celery stalks

2 medium carrots, peeled

Dressing:

2 tablespoons safflower oil

1 tablespoon all purpose flour

1 teaspoon dry mustard

½ cup water

2 teaspoons vinegar

1 large egg, beaten

½ teaspoon salt

¼ teaspoon freshly ground pepper

1 teaspoon sugar

¼ teaspoon cayenne pepper

1. Set the slicing disk to 3mm and fit it into the food processor; secure lid.
2. With the food processor running, push cabbage and celery through the feed tube.
3. Replace slicing disk with the shredding disk (small hole side up); secure lid.
4. With the food processor running, push carrots through the feed tube.
5. Transfer vegetables to a large bowl.
6. In a saucepan over low heat, combine oil, flour and mustard; mix well.
7. Slowly add water, vinegar and egg to the saucepan, whisking constantly.
8. Add remaining ingredients to the saucepan and cook until dressing thickens.
9. Let dressing cool for 15 minutes.
10. Toss cabbage mixture in dressing and let cool completely before serving.

German Cabbage Salad

Ingredients:

½ head of cabbage, cut into pieces

1 medium shallot, peeled

1 small leek (white part only)

½ cup extra-virgin olive oil

½ cup cider vinegar

½ cup sugar

1 tablespoon kosher salt

1 teaspoon caraway seeds

1 teaspoon freshly ground pepper

1. Set the slicing disk to 3mm and fit it into the food processor; secure lid.
2. With the food processor running, push cabbage through the feed tube.
3. Transfer cabbage to a colander; rinse and drain.
4. Adjust the slicing disk to 1mm and secure the lid.
5. With the food processor running, push the shallot and leek through the feed tube.
6. Place the cabbage, shallot and leek into a large bowl; toss well.
7. In a saucepan over medium-high heat, combine oil, vinegar, sugar and salt; mix well.
8. Bring mixture to a boil and cook until the sugar is dissolved.
9. Pour mixture into the bowl with the cabbage mixture.
10. Add remaining ingredients to the bowl; toss well.
11. Cover and refrigerate for 2 hours before serving.

Mediterranean Salad

Ingredients:

1 English cucumber

1 small red onion, halved

3 Roma tomatoes

1 head romaine lettuce

½ cup Kalamata olives, pitted

½ cup Feta cheese, crumbled

Roasted Red Pepper Dressing

1. Set the slicing disk to the widest setting and fit it into the food processor.
2. Secure lid.
3. With the food processor running, push cucumber, onion, tomatoes and lettuce through the feed tube.
4. Transfer sliced ingredients to a bowl; add the olives and feta cheese.
5. Toss with the roasted red pepper dressing (recipe below) and serve.

Roasted Red Pepper Dressing

Ingredients:

1 jar (12 ounces) roasted red peppers, drained

1 teaspoon sugar

3 teaspoons red wine vinegar

2 garlic cloves, peeled

1 small shallot, peeled

1 teaspoon salt

½ teaspoon pepper

1 tablespoon flat leaf parsley

½ cup extra-virgin olive oil

1. Fit food processor with the metal S blade.
2. Place all ingredients, except oil, into the food processor.
3. Secure lid.
4. With the food processor running, drizzle oil through the feed tube.

Crusts Pizzas & Doughs

Flaky Pie Crust

Ingredients:

1 cup unbleached all purpose flour

½ teaspoon kosher salt

½ teaspoon sugar

1 tablespoon sour cream

½ cup unsalted butter, chilled and cut into ½-inch pieces

1 tablespoon ice water

1. For best results, refrigerate all ingredients as well as the food processor bowl and metal S blade for 1 hour prior to preparation.
2. Fit food processor with the metal S blade.
3. Place flour, salt and sugar into the food processor; secure lid and pulse to incorporate.
4. Add remaining ingredients to the food processor; secure lid and pulse 8 times.
5. Remove mixture and form it into a ball.
6. Flatten the ball, wrap it in plastic wrap and chill for 30 minutes.
7. On a lightly floured surface, roll out the dough until 11 inches in diameter.
8. Press dough into a 9-inch pie pan.

Gluten-Free Pizza Crust

Makes 1 pizza

Ingredients:

1 cup white rice flour

¾ cup tapioca flour/starch

3 tablespoons powdered milk

1 tablespoon sugar

1 teaspoon salt

2 teaspoons unflavored gelatin

1 tablespoon xanthan gum

1 teaspoon Italian seasoning

1 tablespoon yeast

2 tablespoons unsalted butter, softened

1 teaspoon apple cider vinegar (not made from grain)

1 large egg, at room temperature

6 ounces lukewarm water (110 degrees)

1. Fit food processor with the metal S blade.
2. Place all ingredients, except butter, vinegar, egg and water, into the food processor.
3. Secure lid and pulse twice.
4. With the food processor running, add remaining ingredients through the feed tube (this will form a dough ball).
5. Transfer dough ball to a bowl, cover and let rise for 45 minutes.
6. Preheat oven to 400 degrees.
7. Rub a pizza pan with oil and place dough in the pizza pan.
8. With the palm of your hand, flatten the dough evenly and make a ridge so the sauce won't spill over (if dough is too sticky, rub hands with rice flour).
9. Let dough rest on the pizza pan for 10 minutes.
10. Place the pizza pan on the lower rack of your oven and bake for 15 minutes.
11. Top the crust with your favorite pizza toppings.
12. Place pizza back in the oven, bake for an additional 15 minutes and serve.

Mike's Caribbean Pizza

Ingredients:

1 cup cooked chicken, cubed

¼ cup sweet BBQ sauce

1 teaspoon jerk seasoning

1 teaspoon lime juice

½ cup plantains, peeled

¼ cup extra-virgin olive oil, divided

1 small onion, peeled

1 red bell pepper, julienned

Pizza dough, 6 ounces (see page 78)

1 cup mozzarella cheese, shredded

2 green onions, chopped

1 tablespoon cilantro leaves, chopped

1. Preheat oven to 450 degrees.
2. In a large bowl, combine chicken, BBQ sauce, jerk seasoning and lime juice; toss.
3. Set the slicing disk to 5mm and fit it into the food processor; secure lid.
4. With the food processor running, push plantains through the feed tube.
5. Heat half of the oil in a skillet over medium heat.
6. Add plantains to the skillet and cook for 3 minutes on each side.
7. Transfer plantains to the chicken mixture.
8. Adjust the slicing disk to 3mm and fit it into the food processor; secure lid.
9. With the food processor running, push onion through the feed tube.
10. Heat the remaining oil in the skillet over medium heat.
11. Add onions to the skillet and cook for 5 minutes or until golden brown.
12. Add the peppers to the skillet and cook for 1 additional minute.
13. Apply non-stick spray to a pizza pan.
14. Stretch the dough across the pizza pan to a 9-inch crust.
15. Top pizza crust with the chicken mixture and sprinkle with cheese.
16. Top pizza with the onion mixture.
17. Bake in the oven for 15 minutes or until golden brown.
18. Top pizza with green onions and cilantro.

Dessert Pizza

Ingredients:

Pizza dough, 12 ounces (see page 78)

½ cup berry preserves

4 ounces cream cheese

3 tablespoons powdered sugar

1 teaspoon lemon juice

½ cup brown sugar

½ cup all purpose flour

¼ cup unsalted butter, chilled and cut into pieces

¼ cup oats

¼ cup pecans

1. Preheat oven to 450 degrees.
2. Apply non-stick spray to a pizza pan.
3. Stretch the pizza dough across the pizza pan, leaving a ½-inch edge all around.
4. Spread the berry preserves over the dough.
5. Fit the food processor with the metal S blade.
6. Place the cream cheese, powdered sugar and lemon juice into the food processor.
7. Secure lid and purée until smooth.
8. Drop cream cheese mixture by spoonfuls around the crust.
9. Place the brown sugar, flour and butter into the food processor; secure lid and pulse.
10. Add the oats and pecans to the food processor; secure lid and pulse to incorporate.
11. Sprinkle crumb mixture over the pizza.
12. Bake pizza in the oven for 20 minutes or until golden brown.

Buffalo Chicken Pizza

Ingredients:

Pizza dough, 6 ounces (see page 78)

1 cup chicken, cooked and chopped

½ cup hot wing sauce

1 cup mozzarella cheese, shredded

½ cup gorgonzola cheese, crumbled

1 carrot, peeled

1 celery stalk

2 green onions, chopped

1. Preheat oven to 450 degrees.
2. Apply non-stick spray to a pizza pan.
3. Stretch the pizza dough across the pizza pan to a 8-inch pizza crust.
4. In a bowl, combine chicken and wing sauce; toss well.
5. Top pizza crust with chicken, mozzarella and gorgonzola cheese.
6. Set the slicing disk to 3mm and fit it into the food processor; secure lid.
7. With the food processor running, push carrot and celery through the feed tube.
8. Top pizza with the sliced vegetables.
9. Bake pizza in the oven for 15 minutes or until golden brown.
10. Top pizza with green onions and serve.

Empanada Dough

Makes 4 to 6 servings

Ingredients:

2 cups unbleached all purpose flour

1 teaspoon salt

½ cup unsalted butter, chilled

6 ounces cream cheese

Beef Empanada Filling (see page 89)

1 large egg

1 teaspoon water

1. Preheat oven to 400 degrees.
2. Line a baking sheet with parchment paper and apply non-stick spray.
3. Fit food processor with the metal S blade.
4. Add flour, salt, butter and cream cheese to the food processor; secure lid.
5. Pulse 8 times and transfer the dough to a lightly floured surface.
6. Kneed the dough, ensuring all ingredients are well combined.
7. Roll the dough until very thin.
8. Using a 4-inch biscuit cutter, cut dough into circles.
9. Place 2 tablespoons of empanada filling on one half of each dough circle, flip other dough half over the filling then crimp the edges to form a pocket.
10. Place empanadas on the prepared baking sheet.
11. In a small bowl, combine egg and water.
12. Brush egg mixture on the empanadas.
13. Place baking sheet in the oven and bake for 20 minutes or until golden brown.
14. Serve immediately.

Pasta Dough

Ingredients:

3½ cups unbleached flour

1 teaspoon kosher salt

3 large eggs

4 large egg yolks

1 teaspoon extra-virgin olive oil

1 tablespoon water

1. Fit food processor with the metal S blade.
2. Place flour and salt into the food processor; secure lid and pulse to incorporate.
3. With the food processor running, push remaining ingredients through the feed tube.
4. Process until a ball forms then continue to process for 30 additional seconds.
5. Rub dough ball with oil and place it into a plastic zipper bag to rest for 30 minutes.
6. To make your favorite pasta such as ravioli, lasagna or tortellini, roll out the dough on a lightly floured surface using a lightly floured rolling pin.
7. Cut the dough into quarters and continue to roll it until you can almost see through the dough.
8. Cut or mold to desired shape.

Pizza Dough

Ingredients:

¼ cup lukewarm water (110 degrees)

1 package active or bread machine yeast

3 cups unbleached all purpose flour

1 teaspoon kosher salt

1 teaspoon sugar

¾ cup water

2 tablespoons extra-virgin olive oil

1. In a bowl, dissolve the yeast in lukewarm water; cover and let rest for 5 minutes.
2. Fit food processor with the metal S blade.
3. Place flour, salt and sugar into the food processor; secure lid and pulse 5 times.
4. Add yeast mixture and remaining water to the food processor; secure lid.
5. While processing, drizzle oil through the feed tube and continue processing until a dough ball forms then process for an additional 1 minute.
6. Transfer dough ball to a lightly floured surface and knead for 1 minute until smooth.
7. Cover dough ball with a damp towel and let rest for 20 minutes.
8. Cut the dough ball into 4 pieces.
9. Roll each piece on the lightly floured surface into a ball until perfectly round.
10. Drizzle some extra olive oil over the dough balls and cover them in plastic wrap.
11. Use immediately or keep refrigerated for up to 2 days.

Cracker Crumb Topping

Ingredients:

1 sleeve (48) salted crackers
1 tablespoon fresh parsley leaves
¼ cup salted butter, melted

1. Fit food processor with the metal S blade.
2. Place crackers into the food processor and secure lid.
3. Process until fine crumbs are achieved.
4. Add parsley to food processor and secure lid.
5. Drizzle butter through the feed tube while pulsing 3 times or until evenly distributed.

Breadcrumb Topping

Ingredients:

8 slices stale white bread
4 tablespoons salted butter, melted
1 tablespoon fresh flat leaf parsley

1. Fit food processor with the metal S blade.
2. Place all ingredients into the food processor and secure lid.
3. Process until evenly combined.

Carb-Free Fried Chicken

Ingredients:

1 whole chicken fryer, cut into 8 pieces

1 cup buttermilk

1 teaspoon salt

6 cups peanut oil

4 cups pork rinds

2 teaspoons poultry seasoning

1. In a large gallon zipper bag, combine chicken, buttermilk and salt.
2. Let marinate overnight.
3. Heat oil in a Dutch oven until it reaches 375 degrees on a thermometer.
4. Fit food processor with the metal S blade.
5. Place remaining ingredients into the food processor; secure lid.
6. Process until fine crumbs are achieved.
7. Spread mixture on a plate.
8. Remove chicken pieces from the zipper bag.
9. Press each chicken piece into the crumb mixture.
10. Gently place chicken into the oil and cook each piece for 12 minutes on each side at 325-350 degrees or until cooked through.
11. Drain on paper towels and serve.

Deb's Tip:
To make a gluten-free coating, use panko made from rice bread or potato flakes.

White Bread

Ingredients:

¼ cup lukewarm water (110 degrees)

1 packet yeast

1 teaspoon sugar

3 cups bread flour

1 teaspoon kosher salt

¾ cup buttermilk

6 tablespoons cold unsalted butter, cut into pieces

1. In a bowl, dissolve the yeast and sugar in the lukewarm water; let proof.
2. Fit food processor with the metal S blade.
3. Place flour and salt into the food processor; secure lid and pulse to combine.
4. With the food processor running, drop the yeast mixture, buttermilk and butter (1 piece at a time) through the feed tube.
5. Process until a dough ball forms then process for an additional 45 seconds.
6. Tug the dough to create a smooth dough ball.
7. Place the ball into a greased bowl; cover with a towel and let rise for 1 hour until it doubles in size.
8. On a lightly floured surface, punch the dough ball down and shape the dough to desired form.
9. Place the dough into a buttered baking pan and let it rest for 45 minutes or until it doubles in size again.
10. Preheat the oven to 400 degrees.
11. Place the bread on the middle rack of the oven.
12. Reduce oven temperature to 350 degrees and bake for 30-35 minutes.

Zucchini Bread

Makes 2 loaves

Ingredients:

¾ cup unsalted butter

1½ cups sugar

4 large eggs

⅔ cup orange juice

2 medium zucchini, ends removed

3⅓ cups all purpose flour

2 tablespoons baking soda

1½ tablespoons salt

½ tablespoon baking powder

1 tablespoon ground cinnamon

1 tablespoon vanilla extract

⅔ cup nuts

⅔ cup raisins

1. Preheat oven to 350 degrees.
2. Apply non-stick spray to 2 loaf pans.
3. Fit food processor with the metal S blade.
4. Add butter, sugar and eggs to food processor; secure lid and process until smooth.
5. Pour orange juice into the food processor.
6. With the metal S blade still in place, add the shredding disk to the food processor and secure lid.
7. With the food processor running, push zucchini through the feed tube.
8. Remove shredding disk.
9. Add remaining ingredients, except raisins, to the food processor.
10. Secure lid and pulse 4 times to combine.
11. Remove the metal S blade and fold in the raisins using a rubber spatula.
12. Divide batter between the loaf pans.
13. Bake in the oven for 1 hour; use a toothpick to test for doneness.

Cheesy Biscuits

Ingredients:

1 piece (4 ounces) sharp cheddar cheese

2 cups self-rising flour

1 teaspoon kosher salt

1 teaspoon sugar

1 stick (½ cup) unsalted butter, chilled and cut into ½-inch pieces

⅔ cup buttermilk

Heavy cream

1. Preheat oven to 400 degrees.
2. Fit the food processor with both the metal S blade and the shredding disk (large hole side up); secure lid.
3. With the food processor running, push cheese through the feed tube.
4. Remove the shredding disk.
5. Add flour, salt, sugar and butter to the food processor.
6. Secure lid and pulse 6 times or until crumbled.
7. Add buttermilk to the food processor and secure lid; pulse 5 times.
8. Transfer dough to a lightly floured surface.
9. Briefly knead the dough, but do not overwork it.
10. Using your hands, push dough to a ¾-inch sheet.
11. Lightly flour a biscuit cutter and cut the dough into biscuits.
12. Place biscuits on a parchment-lined baking sheet.
13. Brush heavy cream on biscuits.
14. Bake in the oven for 10 minutes or until golden brown.
15. Serve warm.

Deb's Tip:
For extra cheesy flavor, sprinkle dough with additional cheddar cheese after brushing it with heavy cream.

Buttery Scones

Ingredients:

2 cups buttermilk biscuit or pancake mix

4 tablespoons unsalted butter, cut into pieces

3 tablespoons sugar

1 teaspoon fresh orange zest

½ cup heavy cream

1 egg yolk

1 teaspoon butter or vanilla extract

1. Preheat oven to 450 degrees.
2. Fit food processor with the metal S blade.
3. Place all ingredients into the food processor; secure lid.
4. Pulse 6 times or until combined and crumbly.
5. Form the dough into a ball.
6. Place dough on a lightly floured surface.
7. Roll dough out until ½-inch thick.
8. Cut dough into triangles using a knife.
9. Place triangles on a parchment-lined baking sheet.
10. Brush each triangle with additional heavy cream.
11. Bake in the oven for 12 minutes or until golden brown.
12. Serve warm.

Meats

Beef Empanada Filling

Ingredients:

1 pound top round beef, cut into 2-inch chunks

½ tablespoon extra-virgin olive oil

½ teaspoon salt

½ teaspoon cumin

1 can (10.5 ounces) tomatoes with green chiles and lime

1 piece (4 ounces) jack cheese

Empanada dough (see page 75)

1. Fit food processor with the metal S blade and secure lid.
2. With the food processor running, push beef chunks through the feed tube.
3. Heat oil in a sauté pan over medium heat.
4. Transfer meat to the pan and break it up using a wooden spoon.
5. Season meat with salt and cumin; brown for 3 minutes.
6. Add the tomatoes to the pan and let simmer for 5 minutes.
7. Replace the metal S blade with the shredding disk (large hole side up); secure lid.
8. With the food processor running, push the cheese through the feed tube.
9. Drain the meat mixture and add the cheese.
10. Finish the empanadas by following the instructions on page 75.

Low Fat Meatloaf

Ingredients:

1 medium onion, peeled and quartered

2 celery stalks

1 medium carrot, peeled

8 mushrooms, cleaned

4 whole grain bread slices

¼ cup beef stock

2 large eggs, beaten

1 teaspoon Worcestershire sauce

¾ pound round steak, cut into 2-inch pieces

¾ pound pork tenderloin, cut into 2-inch pieces

1 teaspoon garlic salt

½ teaspoon freshly ground pepper

¼ cup ketchup

1. Preheat oven to 350 degrees.
2. Fit food processor with the metal S blade.
3. Place onions into the food processor and secure lid; pulse to chop.
4. Apply non-stick spray to a non-stick skillet and preheat over medium heat.
5. Add the onions to the skillet and cook for 3 minutes or until tender; do not brown.
6. Place celery, carrot and mushrooms into the food processor and secure lid; pulse to chop.
7. Add carrot mixture to the skillet and cook for 2 minutes; let cool.
8. Place bread into the food processor and secure lid; process for 1 minute.
9. In a large bowl, combine breadcrumbs, stock, eggs and Worcestershire sauce.
10. With the food processor running, push steak and pork pieces through the feed tube; process until finely chopped.
11. Add onion mixture, meat mixture and remaining ingredients, except ketchup to the breadcrumb bowl mixture.
12. Gently mix by hand until well blended.
13. Transfer meatloaf mixture to a loaf pan and top with ketchup.
14. Place in the oven for 1 hour and serve.

Italian Bolognese Meat Sauce

Ingredients:

1 pound boneless pork chops

1 pound round steak, cut into 2-inch chunks

1 medium onion, peeled and halved

3 garlic cloves

2 tablespoons extra-virgin olive oil

1 teaspoon kosher salt

½ teaspoon freshly ground pepper

½ teaspoon garlic powder

1 can (6 ounces) tomato paste

1 can (28 ounces) petite diced tomatoes

1 can (28 ounces) crushed tomatoes

2 tablespoons red wine

1 sprig fresh thyme

1. Fit food processor with the metal S blade and secure lid.
2. With the food processor running, push pork and steak chunks through the feed tube; remove and set aside.
3. Add onions and garlic to the food processor; secure lid and pulse to chop.
4. Heat oil in a stockpot over medium heat.
5. Add meat and onion mixture to the stockpot; break meat apart using a wooden spoon.
6. Season meat mixture with salt, pepper and garlic powder.
7. Add tomato paste to the stockpot; cook for 5 minutes then reduce heat to low.
8. Add remaining ingredients to the stockpot, cover and cook for 1 hour.
9. Remove thyme and serve over your favorite pasta.

Turkey Italian Sausage

Ingredients:

1 pound turkey breast tenderloins

1 teaspoon fennel seeds

½ teaspoon caraway seeds

½ teaspoon coriander seeds

½ teaspoon kosher salt

½ teaspoon crushed red pepper flakes

¼ teaspoon sugar

1. Fit food processor with the metal S blade.
2. Place all ingredients into the food processor and secure lid.
3. Process for 1 minute or until all the turkey is ground.
4. Form mixture into patties.
5. Cook sausages on a non-stick griddle over medium heat for 3 minutes on each side or until done.

Breakfast Sausage Patties

Ingredients:

1 pound boneless country-style pork ribs

1 teaspoon poultry seasoning

½ teaspoon salt

½ teaspoon paprika

½ teaspoon freshly ground pepper

1. Fit food processor with the metal S blade.
2. Place all ingredients into the food processor and secure lid.
3. Process for 1 minute.
4. Form mixture into patties.
5. Cook patties on a non-stick griddle over medium heat for 3 minutes on each side or until done.

Drinks & Shakes

Berry Shake

Ingredients:

1 pint raspberries, blueberries or strawberries
¼ cup milk
4 scoops berry-flavored ice cream

1. Place all ingredients in the order listed above into a blender; secure lid.
2. Blend on high until smooth and creamy.

Power Protein Shake

Ingredients:

1 cup low-fat milk
2 teaspoons peanut butter (see page 36)
4 scoops chocolate-flavored protein powder
1½ cups ice cubes

1. Place all ingredients in the order listed above into a blender; secure lid.
2. Blend on high until smooth and creamy.

Coffee Frappe

Ingredients:

½ cup brewed espresso, chilled
½ cup heavy cream
4 scoops vanilla ice cream

1. Place all ingredients in the order listed above into a blender; secure lid.
2. Blend on high until smooth and creamy.
3. Add your favorite flavorings like ¼ cup fudge or caramel sauce.

Vanilla Frappe

Ingredients:

1 cup milk
1 teaspoon vanilla extract
4 scoops vanilla ice cream

1. Place all ingredients in the order listed above into a blender; secure lid.
2. Blend on high until smooth and creamy.

Bananas Foster Frappe

Ingredients:

2 ripe bananas, peeled
½ cup milk
⅓ cup caramel topping
5 scoops caramel swirl ice cream

2 ounces spiced rum
Whipped cream
¼ teaspoon ground cinnamon

1. Place all ingredients, except whipped cream and cinnamon, into a blender; secure lid.
2. Blend on high until smooth and creamy.
3. Pour into glasses.
4. Top with whipped cream and cinnamon.

Peppermint Patty Frappe

Ingredients:

½ cup milk
1 teaspoon peppermint extract
5 peppermint candies, crushed
2 tablespoons chocolate syrup
4 scoops vanilla ice cream

1. Place all ingredients in the order listed above into a blender; secure lid.
2. Blend on high until smooth and creamy.

Mangolicious Smoothie

Ingredients:

½ cup concentrated orange juice (not diluted)

1 cup vanilla yogurt

2 cups frozen mango chunks

1. Place all ingredients in the order listed above into a blender; secure lid.
2. Blend on high until smooth and creamy.

Strawberry Papaya Smoothie

Ingredients:

1 cup fresh papaya chunks

1 cup pineapple juice

1 ripe banana

½ cup vanilla yogurt

2 cups frozen strawberries

1. Place all ingredients in the order listed above into a blender; secure lid.
2. Blend on high until smooth and creamy.

Cantaloupe Dream

Ingredients:

2 cups fresh ripe cantaloupe

½ cup orange juice

3 scoops orange sherbet

1. Place all ingredients in the order listed above into a blender; secure lid.
2. Blend on high until smooth and frothy.

Antioxidant Smoothie

Ingredients:

1 cup acai juice or pomegranate juice

½ cup green tea

½ cup yogurt with probiotic cultures

3 cups frozen raspberries or blueberries

1. Place all ingredients in the order listed above into a blender; secure lid.
2. Blend on high until smooth and creamy.

Blue Margaritas

Ingredients:

4 ounces tequila

3 ounces blue Curaçao

1 container (6 ounces) frozen limeade concentrate

½ cup orange juice

5 cups ice cubes

1. Place all ingredients in the order listed above into a blender; secure lid.
2. Blend on high until smooth.
3. Squeeze juice of 1 lime on a plate and spread kosher salt on a separate plate.
4. Dip the rim of the glasses in lime juice then in kosher salt.
5. Divide margarita between glasses and serve with lime wedges.

Peach Bellini

Ingredients:

12 ounces pink champagne

2 ounces peach schnapps

3 cups frozen peaches

1. Place all ingredients in the order listed above into a blender; secure lid.
2. Blend on high until smooth and creamy.
3. Pour into chilled glasses and serve with a peach wedge.

Creamy Pina Colada

Ingredients:

½ cup cream of coconut (sweetened)

½ cup coconut milk

2 ounces pineapple or coconut-flavored rum

3 cups frozen pineapple chunks

1. Place all ingredients in the order listed above into a blender; secure lid.
2. Blend on high until smooth and creamy.

Banana Daiquiris

Ingredients:

2 bananas, peeled

2 tablespoons banana liqueur

2 ounces rum

¼ cup heavy cream

2 cups ice cubes

1. Place all ingredients in the order listed above into a blender; secure lid.
2. Blend on high until smooth and creamy.

Slushy Watermelon Daiquiris

Ingredients:

3 cups watermelon, diced and seeded

2 ounces watermelon-flavored rum or vodka

2 tablespoons sweetened lime juice

2 cups ice cubes

1. Place all ingredients in the order listed above into a blender; secure lid.
2. Blend on high until smooth.

Honeydew Kiwi Supreme

Ingredients:

2 cups ripe honeydew, diced

1 ripe kiwi, diced

6 ounces frozen limeade concentrate (not diluted)

1 cup vanilla yogurt

6 large ice cubes

1. Place all ingredients in the order listed above into a blender; secure lid.
2. Blend on high until smooth and creamy.

Frozen Mudslide

Ingredients:

2 ounces vodka

2 ounces coffee-flavored liqueur

2 ounces Irish cream liqueur

2 tablespoons fudge sauce

4 scoops vanilla ice cream

1. Place all ingredients in the order listed above into a blender; secure lid.
2. Blend on high until smooth and creamy.
3. Serve in chilled glasses.

Frozen Rum Runner

Ingredients:

2 ounces blackberry-flavored brandy

2 ounces banana-flavored liqueur

2 tablespoons grenadine

2 tablespoons sweetened lime juice

5 cups ice cubes

2 ounces dark rum, divided

1. Place all ingredients, except 1 ounce of dark rum, into a blender; secure lid.
2. Blend on high until smooth and creamy.
3. Pour into glasses and float the remaining rum on top.

Cherry Cordial Shake

Ingredients:

1 cup chocolate milk

1 cup frozen cherries

½ cup chocolate fudge sauce

3 cups cherry ice cream

2 ounces chocolate-flavored liqueur (optional)

1. Place all ingredients in the order listed above into a blender; secure lid.
2. Blend on high until smooth and creamy.

Zesty Lime Shake

Ingredients:

1 container (6 ounces) frozen limeade concentrate

1 cup plain yogurt

6 cups ice cubes

1. Place all ingredients in the order listed above into a blender; secure lid.
2. Blend on high until thick and creamy.

Sundae in a Glass

Ingredients:

1 banana, peeled

¼ cup crushed pineapple

5 ripe strawberries

¼ cup fudge sauce

1 cup milk

5 scoops Neapolitan ice cream

1 tablespoon nut topping

2 maraschino cherries

½ candy bar

1. Place all ingredients in the order listed above into a blender; secure lid.
2. Blend on high until smooth and creamy.
3. Serve with whipped cream and a cherry on top.

Chocolate Malt

Ingredients:

¾ cup milk

⅓ cup chocolate syrup

2 tablespoons malted milk powder

5 scoops chocolate ice cream

1. Place all ingredients in the order listed above into a blender; secure lid.
2. Blend on high until smooth and creamy.
3. Serve with whipped cream and a cherry on top.

Desserts

Simple Sugar Cookies

Ingredients:

1 box (18.25 ounces) butter recipe yellow cake mix

½ cup butter-flavored shortening

¼ cup unsalted butter, softened

1 tablespoon orange zest

1 large egg

½ tablespoon granulated sugar

1. Preheat oven to 375 degrees.
2. Fit food processor with the metal S blade.
3. Place cake mix, shortening and butter into the food processor; secure lid.
4. Process for 45 seconds or until smooth.
5. Add remaining ingredients to the food processor; secure lid and pulse to combine.
6. Transfer dough to a lightly floured surface.
7. Divide dough to form 2 balls.
8. Roll out each ball to ⅛-inch thick and cut with desired cookie cutter.
9. Top with sugar and bake in the oven for 8-10 minutes.

Gluten-Free Peanut Butter Cookies

Ingredients:

2 cups roasted peanuts, divided

¼ stick unsalted butter

1½ cups brown sugar

1 teaspoon gluten-free vanilla

1 large egg

2 tablespoons xanthan gum

⅛ teaspoon unbuffered vitamin C crystals (optional)

½ cup semi-sweet chocolate morsels

1. Preheat oven to 350 degrees.
2. Line a baking sheet with parchment paper.
3. Fit food processor with the metal S blade.
4. Place 1½ cups of peanuts, butter and sugar into the food processor.
5. Secure lid and process for 1 minute.
6. Add the vanilla, egg, xanthan gum and vitamin C to the food processor.
7. Secure lid and process for an additional 30 seconds.
8. Add remaining peanuts and chocolate morsels to the food processor.
9. Secure lid and pulse to incorporate.
10. Drop batter by spoonsfuls on a baking sheet, 1-inch apart; press gently on them with a fork.
11. Bake for 15 minutes and serve.

White Chocolate Cheesecake

Crust:
24 vanilla wafers

½ cup white chocolate morsels

Filling:
2 cups white chocolate morsels

1 package (1 ounce) sugar-free white chocolate instant pudding

1 cup heavy cream

2 packages (8 ounces each) cream cheese

2 cups frozen whipped topping, thawed

1. Preheat oven to 350 degrees.
2. Fit a 9-inch springform pan with parchment paper and apply non-stick spray.
3. Fit food processor with the metal S blade.
4. Place crust ingredients into the food processor and secure lid.
5. Process for 1 minute or until crumbly.
6. Press mixture into the prepared springform pan.
7. Bake in the oven for 10 minutes; set aside and let cool.
8. Place all filling ingredients, except whipped topping, into the food processor.
9. Secure lid and process for 2 minutes or until smooth.
10. Remove the metal S blade and fold in the whipped topping using a rubber spatula.
11. Scrape mixture into the baked crust.
12. Chill for 3 hours before serving.

Deb's Tip:
Serve topped with fresh berries.

Creamy Cheesecake

Makes 16 servings

Crust:

24 vanilla wafers

3 tablespoons unsalted butter

¼ cup brown sugar

Filling:

5 packages (8 ounces each) cream cheese

1 cup + 3 tablespoons powdered sugar

1 teaspoon lemon zest

2 teaspoons vanilla extract

2 cups sour cream, divided

4 large eggs

½ cup sugar

1. Preheat oven to 325 degrees.
2. Fit food processor with the metal S blade.
3. Place all crust ingredients into the food processor; secure lid.
4. Process for 1 minute or until fine crumbs are achieved.
5. Line a 9-inch springform pan with parchment paper and apply non-stick spray.
6. Press cookie mixture into the springform pan.
7. Bake in the oven on the center rack for 10 minutes; remove and let cool.
8. Place the cream cheese and powdered sugar into the food processor; secure lid.
9. Process for 2 minutes or until smooth.
10. Add zest, vanilla, 1 cup of sour cream and eggs to the food processor; secure lid.
11. Process for 30 seconds, scrape the sides of the food processor, secure lid and process for an additional 30 seconds.
12. Transfer mixture to the crust.
13. Bake in the oven for 40 minutes.
14. In a bowl, combine remaining sour cream and sugar.
15. Spread sour cream mixture over the cheesecake.
16. Bake in the oven for an additional 10 minutes.
17. Let cool, cover and refrigerate for 4 hours before serving.

Caramel Flan Cheesecake

Ingredients:

1 cup sugar

½ cup water

1 package (8 ounces) cream cheese

1 can (14 ounces) sweetened condensed milk

1 teaspoon vanilla extract

1 teaspoon orange zest

1 cup heavy cream

4 large egg yolks

2 large eggs

1. Preheat oven to 325 degrees.
2. In a microwave-safe bowl, combine sugar and water.
3. Microwave on high for 5 minutes until it turns to caramel.
4. Transfer the caramel to a 9-inch pie pan and cover entire bottom with caramel.
5. Fit food processor with the metal S blade.
6. Add cream cheese and milk to the food processor; secure lid.
7. Purée until smooth.
8. Add remaining ingredients to the food processor; secure lid.
9. Purée for 30 seconds.
10. Pour mixture into the pie pan.
11. Place the pie pan into a larger oven-safe pan filled with water (pie pan should be submerged halfway).
12. Cook in the oven on the center rack for 1 hour.
13. Remove from oven and let rest in the water bath for an additional 30 minutes.
14. Remove pie pan from the water bath and cover with plastic wrap.
15. Chill for 3 hours.
16. Run a knife around the edge of the pan, cover cake with a plate and invert.

Cheesecake Bars

Crust Ingredients:

24 vanilla wafer cookies

3 tablespoons unsalted butter

Cheesecake Ingredients:

4 packages (8 ounces each) cream cheese

1 cup + 2 tablespoons sugar

1 cup sour cream

1 teaspoon lime zest

1 teaspoon vanilla extract

1 tablespoon flour

3 large eggs

1. Preheat oven to 350 degrees.
2. Fit food processor with the metal S blade.
3. Add crust ingredients to the food processor; secure lid and process until smooth.
4. Line a 9x12-inch baking pan with parchment paper and apply non-stick spray.
5. Press crumb mixture into the bottom of the baking pan and bake for 10 minutes.
6. Place cream cheese and sugar into the food processor; secure lid.
7. Process for 2 minutes or until very smooth.
8. Add remaining ingredients, except eggs, to the food processor.
9. Secure lid and process for 1 minute.
10. Using a spatula, scrape the sides to incorporate all of the ingredients; secure lid.
11. With the food processor running, drop eggs (1 at a time) through the feed tube.
12. Pour batter over the prepared crust.
13. Bake in the oven for 45 minutes; use a toothpick to test for doneness.
14. Chill for 3 hours before cutting and serving.

Deb's Tip:
Top the bars with whipped cream and fresh berries.

Banana Dream Pie

Makes 6 servings

Crust Ingredients:

24 vanilla wafer cookies

2 cups banana chips, divided

4 tablespoons unsalted butter

¼ cup brown sugar

Filling:

4 bananas, peeled and sliced

1 teaspoon lemon juice

2 boxes (3.4 ounces each) instant banana pudding

2 packages (8 ounces each) cream cheese

2 cups heavy cream

1 teaspoon banana extract or liqueur

2 cups whipped topping, thawed

1. Preheat oven to 350 degrees.
2. Fit food processor with the metal S blade.
3. Place cookies, 1 cup of banana chips, butter and sugar into the food processor.
4. Secure lid and process for 1 minute or until fine crumbs are achieved.
5. Press cookie mixture into the bottom and sides of a pie plate.
6. Bake crust in the oven for 10 minutes; remove and let cool.
7. In a separate bowl, soak banana slices in lemon juice.
8. For the filling, place pudding mix, cream cheese, cream and banana extract into the food processor; secure lid.
9. Process until smooth and remove the metal S blade from the food processor.
10. Fold banana slices and whipped topping into the cream cheese mixture.
11. Fill crust with the mixture and top with remaining banana chips.
12. Chill for 3 hours before serving.

June's Lemon Delight

Makes 6 to 8 servings

Crust:

1½ sticks unsalted butter, chilled
1½ cups all purpose flour
¼ cup walnuts, chopped

Filling:

1 package (8 ounces) cream cheese
1 cup powdered sugar
1 teaspoon lemon extract
1 cup frozen whipped topping, thawed
1 package (3.4 ounces) instant lemon pudding
3 cups heavy cream

Topping:

2 cups frozen whipped topping, thawed
¼ cup walnuts, chopped

1. Preheat oven to 350 degrees.
2. Fit food processor with the metal S blade.
3. Place all crust ingredients into the food processor and secure lid.
4. Pulse 5 times until coarse.
5. To make the crust, press mixture into a pie pan.
6. Bake crust in the oven for 15 minutes; let cool.
7. Place cream cheese, sugar and lemon extract into the food processor; secure lid.
8. Process for 1 minute then fold in the whipped topping.
9. Transfer mixture to the pie crust and smooth out using a rubber spatula.
10. Place lemon pudding and cream into the food processor.
11. Secure lid and process for 1 minute.
12. Transfer mixture to the pie crust and smooth onto the cream cheese mixture.
13. Top with remaining ingredients.
14. Chill for 3 hours before serving.

Tiramisu

Ingredients:

1 package (1 ounce) sugar-free vanilla pudding

1 package (8 ounces) cream cheese

¾ cup coffee

2 cups whipped topping

16 large marshmallows

1 piece (3 ounces) dark chocolate

35 lady fingers

⅓ cup coffee-flavored liqueur, divided

1. Fit the food processor with the metal S blade.
2. Place pudding mix, cream cheese and coffee into the food processor; secure lid.
3. Process until smooth.
4. Transfer mixture to a large bowl.
5. Using a rubber spatula, fold whipped topping into the cream cheese mixture.
6. In a microwave-safe bowl, microwave marshmallows on high for 6 seconds (the marshmallows should be tripled in size and look like meringue).
7. Using a rubber spatula, fold the marshmallows into the cream cheese mixture.
8. Clean the food processor and fit it with the grating disk; secure lid.
9. With the food processor running, push chocolate through the feed tube.
10. Apply non-stick spray to a 9x13-inch baking dish.
11. Place a layer of lady fingers on the bottom of the baking dish.
12. Drizzle ½ of the coffee liqueur over the lady fingers and top it with ⅓ of the grated chocolate.
13. Top it with ½ of the cream cheese mixture.
14. Top it with another layer of lady fingers and drizzle remaining coffee liqueur.
15. Top with another ⅓ of the grated chocolate.
16. Top with remaining cream cheese mixture and chocolate.
17. Cover with plastic wrap and chill for 3 hours before serving.

Pumpkin Pie with Praline Topping

Makes 8 to 10 servings

Crust:

24 gingersnap cookies

3 tablespoons unsalted butter

¼ cup brown sugar

Cheesecake Filling:

1 package (8 ounces) cream cheese

¼ cup powdered sugar

1 large egg, beaten

½ teaspoon vanilla extract

Pumpkin Filling:

1 can (15 ounces) pumpkin pie filling

¾ cup sugar

2 large eggs

1 teaspoon pumpkin pie spice

1 can (12 ounces) evaporated milk

Praline Topping:

½ cup pecans

⅓ cup unsalted butter

⅓ cup brown sugar

1. Preheat oven to 350 degrees.
2. Fit food processor with the metal S blade.
3. Place all crust ingredients into the food processor and secure lid; process for 1 minute or until crumbly.
4. Line a springform pan with parchment paper and apply non-stick spray.
5. Press mixture into the springform pan.
6. Bake crust in the center of the oven for 10 minutes; let cool.
7. Place cheesecake filling ingredients into the food processor and secure lid.
8. Process for 1 minute.
9. Transfer mixture to the pie crust and smooth out using a rubber spatula.
10. Place pumpkin filling ingredients into the food processor and secure lid.
11. Process for 30 seconds and pour filling into the pie crust.
12. Bake pie in the center of the oven at 350 degrees for 40 minutes.
13. Place praline topping ingredients into the food processor and secure lid.
14. Pulse 4 times.
15. Sprinkle praline mixture over the pie and bake for 10 additional minutes.
16. Let cool at room temperature for 2 hours before serving.

Limeade Pie

Cookie Crust:

40 cookies

¼ cup unsalted butter

½ cup sugar

Pie Ingredients:

1 container (6 ounces) limeade frozen juice concentrate

1 package (8 ounces) cream cheese

1 can (14 ounces) sweetened condensed milk

2 cups heavy cream

1. Preheat oven to 350 degrees.
2. Fit food processor with the metal S blade.
3. Place all crust ingredients into the food processor and secure lid.
4. Process for 2 minutes or until cookies are crushed and evenly mixed.
5. Press mixture into a 9-inch pie pan.
6. Bake in the oven for 10 minutes; let cool.
7. Place limeade, cream cheese and milk into the food processor; secure lid.
8. Process for 1 minute or until smooth.
9. Scrape the sides of the food processor and process for an additional 30 seconds.
10. Transfer mixture to a large bowl.
11. Add heavy cream to the food processor and secure lid.
12. Process for 1 minute or until soft peaks form.
13. Using a rubber spatula, fold the cream into the limeade mixture.
14. Fold mixture into the prepared cookie crust.
15. Chill for 2 hours before serving.

Deb's Tip:
Serve with lime slices.

Deb's Peanut Butter Cup Pie

Crust:

1 package (9 ounces) thin chocolate wafers
4 tablespoons unsalted butter
¼ cup brown sugar

Filling:

1 package (1 ounce) instant vanilla pudding
2 cups heavy cream
2 cups peanut butter
1 cup powdered sugar
1 package (8 ounces) cream cheese
8 peanut butter cup candies, divided
1 container (8 ounces) whipped topping
¼ cup fudge topping for ice cream

1. Preheat oven to 350 degrees.
2. Fit food processor with the metal S blade.
3. Place all crust ingredients into the food processor; secure lid.
4. Process for 1 minute or until fine crumbs are achieved.
5. Press cookie mixture into a 9-inch round pie pan.
6. Bake in the oven on the center rack for 10 minutes; remove and let cool.
7. Place the pudding mix, heavy cream, peanut butter, sugar and cream cheese into the food processor; secure lid and process until smooth.
8. Remove the metal S blade and fold in 4 peanut butter cup candies and the whipped topping using a rubber spatula.
9. Scrape the mixture into the crust and chill for 1 hour.
10. Top cake with fudge topping and remaining peanut butter cup candies.
11. Chill for 2 additional hours before serving.

Brennan's Blueberry Sorbet

Ingredients:

24 ounces frozen blueberries

1 cup simple syrup (see page 140)

1 teaspoon lemon juice

1. Fit food processor with the metal S blade.
2. Place all ingredients into the food processor and secure lid.
3. Process for 4 minutes or until smooth.

Mango Frozen Yogurt

Ingredients:

2 cups frozen mango chunks

½ cup orange juice

¼ cup sugar

1½ cups non-fat plain yogurt

1 teaspoon vanilla extract

1. Fit food processor with the metal S blade.
2. Place all ingredients into the food processor; secure lid.
3. Process until smooth and creamy.

Cranberry Ice Cream

Ingredients:

16 ounces frozen cranberries

1 box (1 ounce) sugar-free white chocolate instant pudding

¾ cup artificial sweetener

2 cups heavy cream

1. Fit food processor with the metal S blade.
2. Place all ingredients into the food processor and secure lid.
3. Process for 2 minutes or until smooth.

Peaches & Cream Ice Cream

Ingredients:

24 ounces frozen peaches

1 package (3.4 ounces) instant vanilla pudding (not dissolved)

2 cups heavy cream

1 cup powdered sugar

2 tablespoons peach schnapps (optional)

4 ounces cream cheese

1. Fit food processor with the metal S blade.
2. Place all ingredients into the food processor; secure lid.
3. Pulse 3 times then process continuously until desired consistency.

Raspberry Sauce

Ingredients:

1 bag (12 ounces) frozen raspberries

⅓ cup sugar

2 tablespoons lemon juice

1. Fit food processor with the metal S blade.
2. Place all ingredients into the food processor and secure lid.
3. Process until smooth.
4. To remove the seeds, strain sauce through a mesh sieve.
5. This sauce is best served over a slice of cheesecake.

Simple Syrup

Ingredients:

¾ cup sugar

¾ cup water

1. In a small saucepan, combine sugar and water.
2. Bring to a boil and stir until all sugar crystals are dissolved.
3. Remove from heat.
4. Let cool to room temperature before using.

Index

Salads

Ahi Tuna Poke Salad 60
German Cabbage Salad 65
Mediterranean Salad 66
Santa Fe Salad with Chicken 56
Tarragon Turkey Salad 58

Seafood

Ahi Tuna Poke Salad 60
Ceviche 18
Salsa Shrimp Dip 20
Smoked Salmon Stuffed Tomatoes 31

Slaws

Asian Slaw 63
Cabbage Slaw with Boiled Dressing 64
Cucumber Radish Slaw 62

Soups

Broccoli Cheddar Soup 49
Carrot Coriander Soup 50
Cream of Spinach Soup 52
Gazpacho 36
Italian Wedding Soup 54
Potato Leek Soup 55
Tomato Soup 53